CONTENTS

THE DIGITAL WORLD

Welcome to a world where your telephone can take a video, your money can be stored on a piece of plastic, and the latest chart music comes from the Internet into your computer in seconds. Welcome to the world of digital technology.

	LAST	CHANGE	P.
NIKKEI	18116.5	+171.8	17
DOW JONES	3319Y2	-8Y1	
FTSE	2452.9	+74.6	
CAC40	1859Y7	+23Y6	
DAX	1584Y5	-2Y0	
		YEN/$	
		YEN/STG	
$/STG	1.7315/1.7309		

▲ This electronic display board shows digital information, in the form of numbers, as well as written information. Each number and letter is made from a grid-like pattern of lights switched on and off by a computer.

'DIGITAL' = 'NUMBERS'

Digital cameras, mobile phones, computers, MP3 music players, CDs (compact discs), DVDs (digital versatile/video discs), calculators, image scanners, email, the Internet – they all do different things. Yet they are all based on digital technology. This means they all handle information in digital form. A digit is another word for a number, like 7 or 3. So digital simply means 'made up of numbers'.

TALKING DIGITAL

Digital is a common 'language' used by the gadgets mentioned above and many more. They all sort, store, change and process their information in the form of numbers. A photograph from a digital camera, a new computer game program, a text message and a song stored in a digital music player are all, in their basic form, long series of numbers.

CHANGING DIGITAL

Digital gadgets and electronic equipment work and communicate with each other using their common digital language. But people find it easier to use pictures, words and sounds. So the gadgets change digital information into forms we can understand and use, like pictures on a screen, sounds coming from earphones or speakers, and words and numbers on a mobile phone display or printed page.

LIVING BY NUMBERS

We cannot really 'see' digital signals themselves – only what they represent, like words and pictures, and the sounds we hear. Often we do not realise we are using digital technology. But it is revolutionising the way we live, work, learn and enjoy ourselves. Why? It is quicker to send emails by computer than to mail letters by post. It is more convenient to use a digital camera when we can alter and print pictures at once, than to use a camera with a photographic film. It is more secure to pay for things by typing in a PIN (personal identification number), than by signing a name which could be forged.

Digital technology can be quicker, safer, more convenient and more secure than traditional ways of doing things.

▲ This mobile phone has a built-in digital camera that stores each photograph as a long series of numbers. It can send the photograph to another mobile phone by transmitting the numbers through the phone network.

FACT FOCUS

DIGITAL FACTS

- Over one-half of all the telephones in the world are mobiles, most of them using digital technology.

- Around 210 countries are connected to the Internet. Fewer than 20 are not.

- Tens of billions of emails are sent around the world each day.

- A typical DVD can store 9 gigabytes of information – enough to hold all the words in the Bible 10,000 times.

- Most digital cameras can recognise more than 16 million different colours.

- All the fibre-optic cables laid so far to carry digital signals, joined end to end, would go around the world 5,000 times.

DIGITAL INFORMATION

When you send someone an email, the message you type zips around the world not as letters and words, but as a long series of numbers. How does a piece of digital technology like a computer change your words into digits? The process is called 'digitising information'.

CHANGING INTO NUMBERS

Any kind of information – words, pictures, lists, sums, sounds – can be turned into numbers. It is like using a code. Imagine trying to make a secret message using numbers to represent letters. Suppose A is 1, B is 2, C is 3 and so on. Then you could replace the letters in the word DIGITAL with their numbers, with D as 4, I as 9, continuing to L which is 12. Using this code we can turn information in one form, as the written word DIGITAL, into digital information, as numbers – in this case 4-9-7-9-20-1-12.

BINARY CODE

Digital technology goes a step further. It does not store information in the form of the ten digits (single numbers) we usually use – 0, 1, 2 and so on, through to 9. This ten-digit system

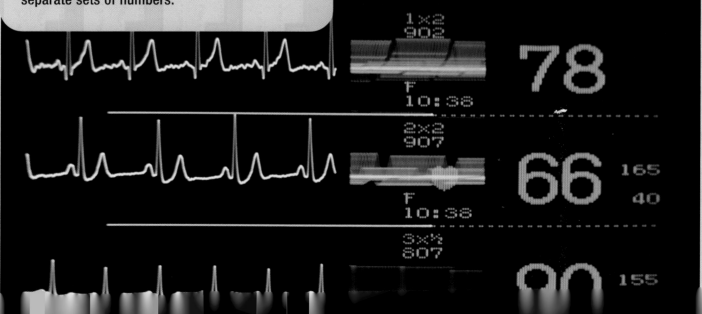

▼ This display shows information in two ways. One is digital, using numbers which change now and then as the information alters. The other form is wavy lines that change continuously as they go up and down, which is called analogue.

FACT FOCUS

DIGITAL VS ANALOGUE

Information in analogue form is very different from digital information. Analogue information varies continuously, changing in a smooth way, like up-and-down waves. It is shown by hands on dials and pointers on gauges, and as wave-like moving traces. Digital information is not continuous. It is split into chunks and stored as separate sets of numbers.

is called decimal. In the decimal system, each digit to the left of another digit is ten times the value. So the decimal number 111 means, from right to left, 1 one, 1 ten and 1 hundred.

Digital technology does not use decimal, it uses binary. The binary system has just two digits, 0 and 1, or zero and one. In the binary system, each digit to the left of another digit is only twice the value. So the binary number 111, again reading it from right to left, means 1 one, 1 two and 1 four. We would write this in the decimal system as 1 + 2 + 4, which is 7.

ON AND OFF

Inside computers and other kinds of digital equipment are millions of tiny switching devices called transistors or gates. These can be either 'on' or 'off'. 'On' is a binary 1, when a tiny pulse of electricity flows. 'Off' is a binary 0, when no electricity flows. So any form of information can be digitised by changing it into binary, and then representing it inside a digital machine such as a computer as pulses and no-pulses of electricity.

▼ Long before computers were invented, the binary system of numbers was described by Gottfried Wilhelm Leibniz (1646–1716). He made many important advances in science, especially mathematics, and developed one of the first mechanical calculators which could add, subtract and multiply.

23 in DECIMAL   2 tens   3 ones

23 in BINARY   1 sixteen   1 four   1 two   1 one

23 as ON/OFF SWITCHES

▲ The decimal number 23 is 3 ones and 2 tens. It can also be represented in binary as 00010111, which (from right to left) is 1 one, 1 two, 1 four, 0 eights and 1 sixteen. In turn this can be represented by switches which are either ON (1) or OFF (0). In a computer the switches are microscopic transistors.

'DIGITAL' IN BINARY

In binary, each of the 0s and 1s is called a bit, which is short for 'binary digit'. A group of bits, usually eight, is known as a byte. If we use one byte to represent each letter of the word DIGITAL, then it changes from 4-9-7-9-20-1-12 in decimal to 00000100-00001001-00000111-00001001-00010100-00000001-00001100 in binary. Digital equipment such as computers handle this kind of information as on-off pulses of electricity.

HANDLING
DIGITAL

Most of the electronic gadgets we use every day have microchips inside them. These chips make it easy to process, store and transmit vast amounts of digital information.

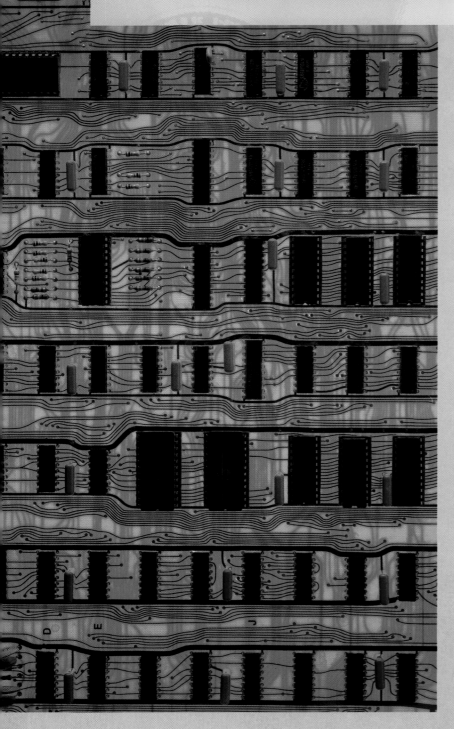

CHIPS FOR DIGITAL

Microchips are small wafer-like pieces or 'chips', usually made of the substance silicon. Each contains thousands or millions of microscopic electronic devices such as transistors and resistors, all connected together in what is called an integrated circuit, IC. The chip sends, receives, stores and alters the pulses of electricity which are digital information or data (see page 12). Microprocessors are more powerful microchips; they are the electronic 'brains' that are found in computers and many other types of electronic equipment.

PROCESSING DIGITAL DATA

Processing information means altering it and turning it into other forms. A computer processes its information by comparing different groups of bits (0s and 1s) in different parts of its memory, and by using simple mathematics to change some of the bits into others. The bits can represent words, sounds, pictures or any other type of information.

◀ These 'black boxes', shown actual size, are plastic cases containing microchips buzzing with digital information. Chips like these can store information in digital form and alter or process it into other forms.

▲ The tiniest speck of dust or droplet of water can ruin a microchip as it is made. So chips are produced in 'clean rooms' where workers wear head-to-toe suits that keep in dust from their clothes, skin and hair. The face masks trap moisture from their breath.

HISTORY FOCUS

FIRST MICROPROCESSORS
In 1971 the Intel company needed to design several different microchips for a range of electronic calculators. But engineer Ted Hoff (1937–) suggested making one general-purpose chip for all the different calculators. The result was the Intel 4004, the first microprocessor, which was about the size of your little fingernail. Microprocessors are now in endless machines and gadgets, from toys and mobile phones to toasters and washing machines.

STORING DIGITAL DATA
Information stored in digital electronic form takes up less space than information in other forms, such as on paper. You would need about ten shelves to store 1,000 copies of this book. But turn all the book's words and pictures into digital form and they become around half a million bits. Then you could fit the 1,000 copies in digital form onto one CD (compact disc).

TRANSMITTING DIGITAL DATA
Information is usually more compact when in digital form, so it can be sent from place to place quickly and reliably. The Internet, mobile phones, digital radio and digital television all work in this way. Their information is in the form of long strings of binary digits, 0s and 1s. It is easy to send these bits in sequence, from one piece of digital technology to another, even right around the world.

DIGITAL MEMORIES

Digital devices such as computers have enormously powerful memories that can store almost any kind of information. The two most common kinds of memory are microchips and hard drives.

THE NEED FOR MEMORY

Without reliable memories, computers would be useless. When you write a letter using a computer, its memory stores the words as you type them. Computers are not the only things that have memories. A digital alarm clock remembers the time you set for the alarm. Most telephones have memories to store the numbers you call most often.

MICROCHIP MEMORIES

Microwave ovens, cars and many other machines have memories like these. They are usually in the form of tiny microchips, as

▲ It takes an enormous amount of space to store information as books, as in this library in Weimar, Germany. Information stored digitally in computers takes up much less space. Looking for it using electronic word searches can also be easier.

shown on page 10. Inside a chip are thousands or even millions of microscopic switches called transistors. Each transistor can be either 'on' or 'off'. When it is switched on, it stores the bit (binary digit) 1. When it is off, it stores the bit 0. Working together, many of these transistors can store long strings of bits, and so store digital information.

Hard drives

A microchip can store millions of bits which usually represent written characters – letters, numbers and symbols like +, * and &. But computers need to store much more information than this. So most computers have larger memory devices called hard drives. A big hard drive can store as much as 200 gigabytes – enough memory to hold all the words in all the books in a typical public library. But the size of this hard drive is only about the size of one book.

A hard drive has a pile or stack of discs, called platters, made from magnetic material. Automatic 'arms' carrying read/write heads move across the platters, like the old-fashioned needle of a vinyl record player. They can store or 'write' information onto each platter by magnetising a tiny area of it, using one pattern of magnetism to store a binary 1 and a different pattern to store a binary 0. The arms

can also retrieve or 'read' information from the platters by detecting the patches of magnetism already there. The platters spin round at about 270 kilometres per hour – faster than a sports car at top speed!

HISTORY FOCUS

INVENTING NOTHING
Long ago there was no number or symbol for zero, 0. People just left a blank space to indicate 'nothing'. The zero as we use it today probably began about 1,500 years ago with the Hindu people of the Indian region. But archaeologists now believe that a form of zero was in use long before, more than 2,200 years ago in Babylonia. Without the invention of the zero, the binary system used by computers and other digital machines would not be possible.

▼ A huge amount of information is now available in digital form. Every CD and DVD in this shop is packed with billions of binary digits or bits.

CDS AND DVDS

Small shiny discs that can store books, films and music – such an idea would have seemed impossible fifty years ago. Today, thanks to digital technology, we have CDs (compact discs) and DVDs (digital versatile/video discs).

▲ This photograph, taken with an electron microscope, shows the surface of a compact disc magnified more than 2,000 times. The pits (bowl-like hollows) and lands (flat areas) store binary digits or bits of information – 0s and 1s.

INSIDE A DISC

CDs and DVDs look and work the same way. They are made from a thin disc of aluminium coated with tough clear plastic. Information is stored digitally on the disc as a spiral shape or pathway of microscopic bowl-like pits and flat patches in the aluminium. Each pit represents a binary 1 and each flat area or land represents a 0. Unwound, the whole spiral would be nearly six kilometres long.

A DVD can store at least seven times more information than a CD because its pits and lands are smaller and closer. Most DVDs have a storage capacity of around nine gigabytes, 9 GB – enough to hold a complete movie or thousands of pages of written words.

STORING MUSIC ON DISC

How can these discs store music and pictures? Music is made of sounds called notes. Each note has a certain frequency (high or low pitch), amplitude (high or low volume) and duration (length of time). To store music on a compact disc, the music must be sampled – a process that turns musical notes into binary digits, as strings of 0s and 1s.

SAMPLING

Thousands of times each second, electronic equipment measures or 'samples' all the sounds in the music – their frequency and amplitude. The results are stored as numbers. The faster this happens, which is called the sampling rate, the more closely the strings of numbers will resemble the original music. But a faster sampling rate also creates more digits that need more room on the disc to store them. For most music CDs the sampling rate is 44,100 times per second.

When the entire piece of music has been sampled, it ends up as a gigantic sequence of binary digits, 0s and 1s. This is fed from the sampling machine to a laser beam which 'burns' the binary digits onto the compact disc, as pits with lands between them.

CD STORAGE CAPACITY

A typical CD stores around 5,000 million (five billion) bits of digital information. Each bit occupies an area roughly two millionths of a millionth of a square metre. Suppose you could enlarge the CD so that each pit was as big as your thumbnail. Then the entire CD would cover a circular area about five kilometres across.

▼ Inside a CD or DVD player, a laser beam scans across the disc and reads the pattern of pits and lands. Electronic circuits turn this pattern first into electrical pulses which represent strings of binary 0s and 1s, then into varying electrical signals, and then into sound frequencies from the loudspeaker.

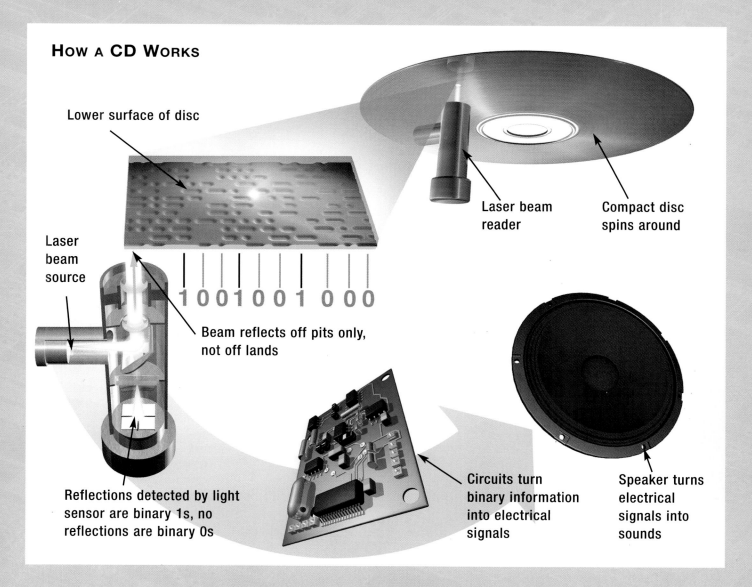

HOW A CD WORKS

Lower surface of disc

Laser beam source

1 0 0 1 0 0 1 0 0 0

Beam reflects off pits only, not off lands

Laser beam reader

Compact disc spins around

Reflections detected by light sensor are binary 1s, no reflections are binary 0s

Circuits turn binary information into electrical signals

Speaker turns electrical signals into sounds

DIGITAL MUSIC PLAYERS

CD players were revolutionary when they were invented in the 1980s. But the latest portable music players can store even more sounds in even less space, making it easy for people to listen to a greater choice of music anywhere and at any time.

MP3 PLAYERS

An MP3 player is a tiny computer that specialises in playing music. It has all the key components of any computer: a memory, a processor, input and output. The input is a cable you connect from your computer to the player to copy music as songs or tracks. Each song is in the form of a computer file consisting of millions of binary digits.

Different MP3 players have different kinds of memory for storing these files. Players that store thousands of songs have a hard drive like the one in a computer but much smaller. Players with more limited storage have microchip memories, and the whole player can be the size of your little finger.

OUTPUTS

The 'brain' of an MP3 player is a microprocessor that reads the binary digits and turns them into an output of electrical signals. The signals go to the earphones, which change them into the sound waves you can hear. Most MP3 players have another form of output too. This is a small visual display that shows you which track is playing, its title, the names of the musicians and other information.

▲ An almost finger-sized digital music player can hold the same number of tracks as a large suitcase of CDs. This makes it easy for people to take huge amounts of music with them, wherever they go.

▲ This mixing desk in a recording studio not only turns the sounds of an orchestra into digital computer files. It can also change the sound from each instrument, and combine or 'mix' the sounds from all the instruments in different ways, by altering the digital signals from them.

MP3 FILES

How can a tiny portable music player store all the music from hundreds of CDs? The answer lies in the MP3 files that it uses. To put the music from a CD onto an MP3 player, you first have to copy or 'rip' the music from the CD onto your computer. Each track on the CD is stored in the computer in a format called MP3. This format compresses or 'squeezes' the information. So the MP3 file is up to 16 times smaller, in terms of the number of bits, than the same information on the CD. You can rip songs in various ways to make larger or smaller MP3 files. The smaller the file, the more details are lost during the ripping process, which means the sound quality is poorer.

HISTORY FOCUS

NAUGHTY NAPSTER
In June 1999 Shawn Fanning, then a student in the USA, caused controversy when he developed a computer program called Napster. It allowed people to share copies of MP3 computer files that they had made from their own music CDs, by sending them over the Internet – something that is normally illegal. Record companies sued Napster for breaking copyright laws and forced it to close in 2001. Since then Napster has started up again, but it now sells MP3 tracks legally over the Internet.

SMART CARDS

Imagine a small piece of plastic that can open your front door, pay for shopping, top up your mobile phone and help you borrow library books. Using digital technology, smart cards can make our lives simpler and our personal information more secure.

WHAT ARE SMART CARDS?

Old-fashioned credit and cash cards have magnetic strips on the back that store the basic details of a person's bank account. Although smart cards look similar and usually have magnetic strips, they also have a small computer chip. The built-in chip can store much more information than the magnetic strip, for many different purposes. Information is recorded digitally in a secure encrypted form – as a secret code. This makes it hard for criminals to use or steal the information.

HOW SMART CARDS WORK

To use a smart card, you usually have to place it in or on a special reader device. In a supermarket, you push a 'chip-and-pin' smart card into the checkout terminal reader. The reader connects to the computer chip in the card and gets your details. You punch in your PIN and the reader checks the numbers against the information stored securely on your card. If the details match, the checkout reads your bank details from the smart card and charges the cost of your shopping to your account.

USES OF SMART CARDS

So far, the biggest use for smart cards has been in replacing old-style credit and debit cards. But they have many other uses. Most people carry a wallet or purse with credit cards, cash cards, library cards, club membership cards,

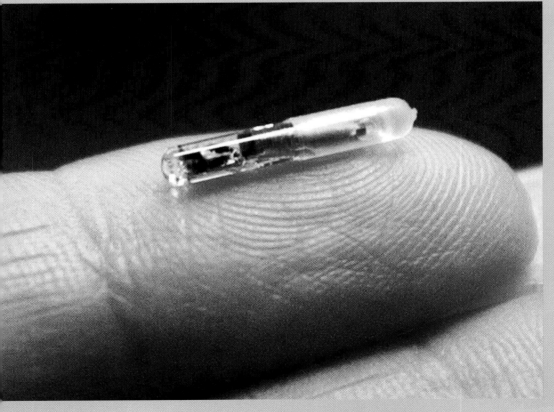

◄ People could soon carry digital information inside their bodies. A tiny memory device put under the skin may store our medical details. Then doctors can 'read' them by radio in an emergency, such as after an accident, when a blood transfusion is needed.

SIM CARDS
If you have a mobile phone, it probably has a smart card called a SIM (subscriber identification module) inside. This is similar to an electronic key. It unlocks the telephone, tells it who you are, and allows you to use the phone network to make calls. It can also store names, addresses and numbers. You can take the SIM card out of one phone and plug it into another one, taking all your personal information, phone numbers and remaining credit with you.

▼ A SIM card is a tiny computer memory that stores your personal information inside your mobile phone. It can hold thousands of bytes of information – enough for hundreds of telephone numbers.

▲ Smart cards can be electronic 'keys'. The card and the reader, or 'lock', can be programmed so that only certain cards can open the door at certain times. Also every use can be recorded for security.

mobile phone top-up cards and similar items – and all could be replaced by a single smart card. Some schools and colleges give students smart cards that work as door keys, computer access cards, library cards and bus passes. The cards may also operate as cash cards in the college's vending machines and cafés.

GOING PLACES
Transport is another smart card application. On buses and trains, in taxis and planes, carrying cash can be inconvenient for some passengers. Smart cards are becoming a popular way to pay the fare. Certain cities charge drivers automatically as they go along roads, over bridges and through tunnels, using smart cards stuck to the vehicle windscreen. Smart cards can also be used as identity cards, medical cards and organ-transplant cards.

DIGITAL IMAGES

Computers can work with pictures just as easily as with words. Digital images are pictures stored as binary digits (bits) – 0s and 1s. Once pictures are in digital form, you can easily load them into a computer, change or edit them, email them and print them.

PHOTOS BY NUMBERS

A traditional camera records pictures on a roll of photographic film inside. Chemicals in the film react to light rays streaming into the lens and record a recognisable picture. Open up a digital camera and you will not find a film. Instead, behind the lens is a grid or matrix of light-detecting cells. This is called a charge-coupled device, CCD.

ELECTRONIC EYE

The CCD is an electronic version of our eyes. It breaks the picture captured by the lens into millions of tiny units called pixels. A computer chip inside the camera measures the colour and brightness of each pixel and represents this information as numbers. So a digital photograph is really a long string of binary numbers, 0s and 1s, each representing the colour and brightness of one tiny part of the image. The smaller and more numerous the pixels, the clearer and sharper the overall photograph. In a normal-sized photo, each pixel is about 200 times smaller than the head of a pin.

◀ Digital cameras can be far smaller than ordinary cameras because the light-sensitive chip or CCD is smaller than photographic film. This miniature digital camera can be easily hidden, to take photographs secretly.

EDITING DIGITAL PHOTOS

Images are easy to alter or edit in digital form. Suppose you want to flip a photograph from left to right, as if seen in a mirror. Your computer takes the numbers representing the pixels along each horizontal line of the photograph and simply reverses them – puts them in the opposite order. What if you want to make a photograph brighter? Your computer looks at the brightness value for each pixel and increases the number slightly. If you 'crop' a photo (select part of it), the computer keeps the numbers representing the area of the image you want, and deletes the rest.

▼ Medical scanners send their information to a computer as a stream of binary digits. The computer converts these to an image displayed on a screen. Different parts of the image can be coloured or highlighted to make it easier for doctors to identify any problems.

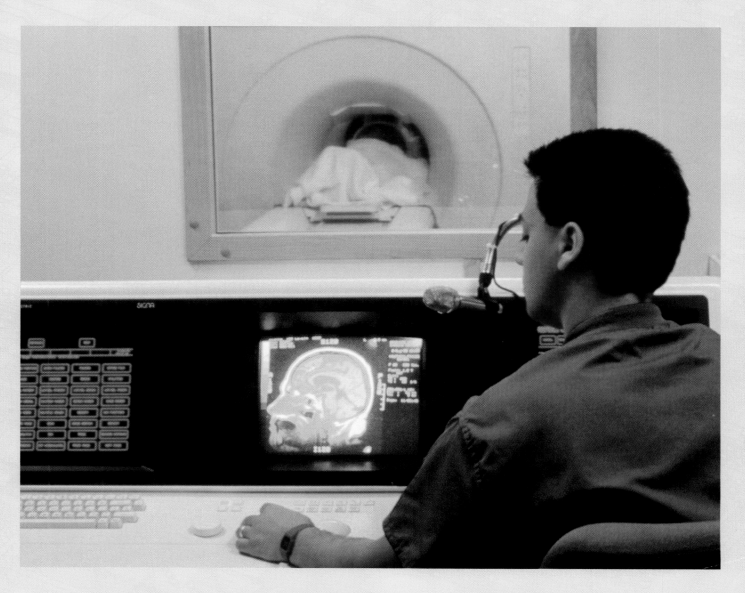

COMPUTER-AIDED DESIGN

Many of the products we use every day are made using digital technology. Thanks to computer-aided design (CAD) and computer-aided manufacturing (CAM), a new product can go all the way from the drawing board to the production line in digital form.

WHAT IS CAD?

CAD is a way of making precise drawings using a computer. It is a very advanced version of the ordinary paint packages or graphics programs you might use on a computer at home or school. CAD drawings store the shape of a complex, three-dimensional object in digital form. You can edit it on screen, rotate it or view it from any angle, and zoom in to show more detail. CAD drawings are also used to make items like clothes using computer-aided manufacturing. The output from the CAD program can operate lasers and other machines that cut, weave or stitch cloth to the original pattern, with little human help.

▲ Almost any product can be designed digitally, even a training shoe. The CAD program transforms a curved object like the trainer's wrap-around heel into a flat shape which can be cut from a sheet.

CAD IN ACTION

Almost every car, ship and aeroplane today is designed using CAD. Architects also use CAD for new buildings. CAD makes it quicker, easier, and cheaper for creative people to try out new designs without having to redraw their work many times. They can send their designs to colleagues over the Internet and email them directly to the factory so that manufacturing can start at once.

DIGITAL WIND

Engineers used to test the streamlined shapes of new planes, cars, boats and trains by putting small-scale models in wind tunnels. This was slow, complex and costly.

Today, these tests are done with computers. The computer carries out ultra-fast calculations of how the air moves, and works out how it will flow around the aeroplane or other object. All the testing relies on digital technology, as computers juggle billions of numbers.

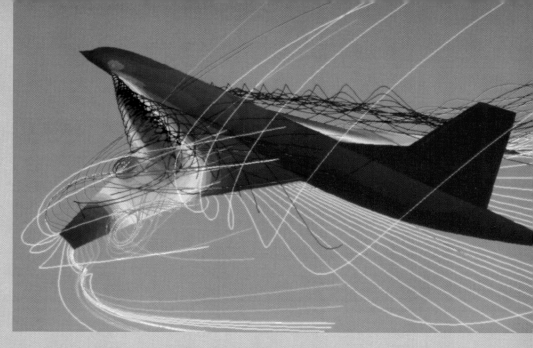

▲ A computer shows how air rushing past a new supersonic aeroplane will heat up its different parts. Red is hottest and blue is coldest, so the plane's wings will heat up much more than its body.

EVIDENCE FOCUS

REDESIGN YOUR ROOM

If you have a computer graphics program, try drawing a plan of your bedroom on screen. Draw the basic floor plan first and then put in the furniture afterwards. Now try moving the furniture by drawing it in different places. Can you come up with a better layout for your room? You could try the same with other rooms or with your garden.

▼ This hi-tech machine is an enormous pair of 'digital scissors'. A laser beam, controlled by a CAD program in a computer, moves across the cloth and cuts out shapes very quickly and accurately.

MOVIES AND SPECIAL EFFECTS

Digital technology makes it quicker and cheaper to develop breathtaking movies and animations. It is possible to create scenes and effects that people never dreamed of when movies were first invented, just over a hundred years ago.

LIGHTS, CAMERA... DIGITAL ACTION!

A movie or film is a series of many still photos called frames, each one slightly different from the last. When our eyes see the frames at high speed, our brains are tricked into seeing a moving picture. Digital technology makes it

▼ In a computer-generated movie like *Madagascar*, everything from the shape of a character's body to the expression on its face can be altered, simply by changing the numbers that represent them in digital form inside a computer.

easier to put movies together by storing each separate frame as a digital image. You can produce a digital movie using two methods. One is by making it in the traditional form using reels of photographic film, and then converting these into digital form. The other method is using a digital video camera that stores frames digitally from the beginning.

EDITING

Once the film is digital, you can edit each frame like a separate digital photograph. You can add special effects, such as explosions,

using computer graphics. Or you can combine scenes of modern-day actors with historical scenes from many years ago.

DIGITAL ANIMATION

Digital technology can also be used to make computer-generated imagery (CGI). Where artists once used pens and paper to draw cartoons and animations, now they are more likely to use digital equipment similar to CAD (see page 22). They produce the basic designs for the characters and backgrounds, such as street scenes or trees, and draw the first and last frame in a sequence, all on the computer. The computer then fills in the missing frames by working out, mathematically, all the steps in between.

MORPHING

Morphing – slowly transforming one image into a very different one – works in the same way. You feed the computer two photographs, perhaps one of a person's face and the other of a monkey's face. The computer digitises them. It then works out how to change the first series of numbers stage by stage into the second. This is called digital image processing. It can also mix real-life scenes with computer-generated images.

▲ Characters in movies such as *Monsters, Inc.* are animated using 'wire-frames'. These are points and lines drawn on a grid, like three-dimensional graph paper. The characters can be moved about by moving the points from one grid location to another.

HISTORY FOCUS

MONSTERS, INC.
Making the film *Monsters, Inc.* (2001) was a digital challenge for the Disney and Pixar studios. It involved processing huge amounts of data with enormously powerful computers.

- The film contains around 130,000 frames.

- Each frame was made from separate computer drawings, added together in layers one on top of another.

- There are between five and 200 layers in every frame.

- Pixar's computer animation artists used 250 powerful computer workstations, each containing eight microprocessors, to design the film.

- The movie generated around 25 trillion bytes of digital data – enough to fill the hard drives of about 800 ordinary computers.

DIGITAL MUSIC

Music is one of the greatest achievements of the creative human mind. Musicians now use digital technology to generate sounds, compose music and edit the recordings they make.

MAKING DIGITAL MUSIC

Some musicians feel digital technology lets them be more creative. One musician can compose, play and record an entire orchestral composition using just one instrument – a synthesiser. This is a computerised electronic keyboard able to make any sound you can imagine. Some musicians have experimented with entirely new forms of digital instruments, such as digital electronic cellos, guitars, violins and harps.

ALTERED INSTRUMENTS

When you stroke the strings of an electronic violin with a bow, a microchip inside translates the notes you play into streams of binary digits. This information travels to a synthesiser attached to the violin, which plays an electronic sound for that note. But it does not have to be a violin sound. The synthesiser can take the basic digital information from the violin and create a sound like a trumpet, a piano or an imaginary new instrument.

◄ Musicians like Wyclef Jean (left) are now recording their music digitally so that fans can access it directly over the Internet. The technology for broadcasting sounds, animations and movies over the Internet is called streaming media.

SAMPLING MUSIC

Samplers are electronic instruments that record everyday sounds and play them back in unexpected ways. You can record a dog barking and then play that noise back using a keyboard. The sampler works by changing the dog bark into a pattern of binary digits. When you press different keys on the keyboard, a computer chip inside transforms these mathematically, for example, to make barks of higher or lower pitch.

COMPOSING DIGITAL MUSIC

Many musicians make up or compose music by experimenting on a keyboard or guitar, then writing out the notes on paper. The task of writing down or transcribing music is skilled and complex. A popular computer program called Sibelius can do this automatically. It recognises the sounds being played, turns them into a digital form, and works out which notes they represent. It then writes the results in proper musical notation, as notes on the lines of the musical stave.

▼ Any sounds, including human voices, can be picked up by microphones and digitised – turned into long strings of binary numbers, 0s and 1s. Musicians often record their songs and other work using a special type of magnetic tape called DAT, digital audio tape.

MOBILE PHONES

At the last count, there were more than 1,300 million mobile (cellular) phones in the world. They use digital technology to send and receive text messages, data, photographs, videos and even television – as well as voice conversations.

DIGITAL PHONES

At its heart, a mobile phone is more like a computer than an old-style telephone. Inside your mobile is a small microprocessor chip linked to a radio transmitter and receiver. When you make a call, the microprocessor turns your voice into binary digits and the radio transmitter beams them through the air as digital signals in the form of radio waves. The signals are picked up by a nearby mast, enter the main telecom network, and are broadcast and detected by the mobile of the person you call. In that person's phone the receiver picks up the signals, and the microprocessor turns them back into sounds.

▲ Thanks to digital technology, mobile phones are much more than gadgets for talking to your friends. The latest handsets can play games, take photos, store and play MP3 music files and even receive digital television pictures.

EVIDENCE FOCUS

SPEAKING MOBILE LANGUAGE

You will need a mobile phone and a radio. Make sure the radio and the phone are switched off. Switch on the radio, to the AM waveband if possible. Put the phone near the radio and switch it on. You should hear a pattern of pulsing noises from the radio. The phone is 'talking' to the mobile network by sending out radio waves, which the radio detects. The mobile phone is effectively saying: 'Hello, I am switching on and ready to start receiving calls.'

THE WORLD AT YOUR FINGERTIPS

Mobile phones have made life more convenient, allowing people to talk to each other wherever and whenever they want. Digital technology lets a mobile phone do much more. It can send and receive text messages, which are transmitted in digital form. Many mobile phones have a tiny, built-in digital camera that can take photos or videos and send them to other mobile phones or computers.

MORE EXTRAS

Many modern mobiles can browse parts of the Internet, showing simple pages from the World Wide Web. Some mobiles can send emails. Some can receive television pictures, almost like a TV set. The digital signals for these pictures are broadcast specially for mobile phones, on a different network from the main digital television network.

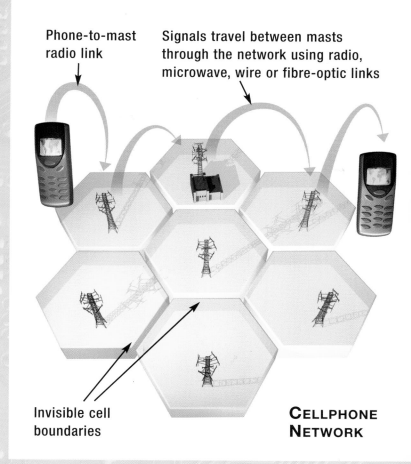

Phone-to-mast radio link

Signals travel between masts through the network using radio, microwave, wire or fibre-optic links

Invisible cell boundaries

CELLPHONE NETWORK

▼ Dish and other aerials on tall buildings or masts send and receive mobile phone calls, as digital signals in the form of radio waves. The dishes belong to different mobile providers and point in various directions. Radio signals travel almost instantly because they move at the speed of light – 300,000 kilometres per second.

▲ Mobile phones are called cellphones because they use a system of invisible, hexagon-shaped areas called cells. Each cell has its own transmitter/receiver mast that communicates with all the phones near it and with the general telecom network. If you make a call while travelling and you cross a cell boundary, the radio signals switch automatically from one cell's mast to the next.

THE INTERNET

There is no better demonstration of the power of digital technology than the Internet. This worldwide communications network allows people to share words, pictures, sounds and even movies using their computers.

THE SIZE OF THE INTERNET

The Internet or 'Net' is the physical network of computers and the connections between them. The Net began as a project to link four large computers at American universities in the 1960s. Now it connects almost 1,000 million personal computers worldwide, as well as computer networks in governments, schools, colleges and businesses.

PACKETS

Information races back and forth over the Net in the form of tiny 'packets' of digital data. When you send an email, it is split into many of these digital packets. The packets make separate journeys through the network, sometimes by very different routes – going

▲ Cybercafés make it easy for travellers to keep in touch by using the Internet to send emails and messages. Webcams – small digital cameras mounted on top of each computer – allow people to send pictures of themselves to friends and relatives.

across different continents or up and down to different satellites. At the destination the packets are put back together again. Sending information by this kind of 'packet switching' is very efficient, especially if part of the network is damaged or not working.

THE WORLD WIDE WEB

One of the Internet's most useful parts is the World Wide Web (www). The Web is a way of putting information in digital form on one computer, a Web server, so that other computers, running programs called Web browsers, can share it. Unlike the pages of a book, the digital information on the Web can be instantly updated, and each page can be linked to many other pages. With millions of computers involved, the result is a worldwide library of information which is available at any time, and mostly for free.

INFORMATION SUPERHIGHWAY

Emails and Web pages travel around the Net in the way that cars and trucks travel along the biggest, fastest roads. This is why the Net is sometimes called the 'information superhighway'. Receiving information from the Net into your computer is called downloading. Sending information from your computer out through the Net is known as uploading.

▶ People of all ages can use the Internet. In schools like this one, pupils use the network to talk to children in other countries. This helps them to learn about languages and cultures around the world.

◀ Tim Berners-Lee is the 'guiding hand' behind the World Wide Web. In 1994 he became director of the World Wide Web Consortium (W3C), which helps to manage the way the Web develops.

HISTORY FOCUS

INVENTING THE WEB

British computer scientist Sir Tim Berners-Lee (1955–) invented the World Wide Web in the late 1980s, to help scientists share their research. People soon started using it to share all kinds of information. Berners-Lee says that he always had in mind helping people. 'I designed it for a social effect – to help people work together – and not as a technical toy.'

DIGITAL
BROADCASTING

Digital television and radio are increasingly popular.
They offer a bigger choice of programmes, and better
quality pictures and sound, than old-style broadcasting.
They transmit programmes to your TV or radio as an
ultra-fast stream of binary digits.

PRE-DIGITAL RADIO

When you tune in an old-style
radio, its aerial picks up radio
waves coming through the air,
which are turned into sound
waves you can hear. But hills,
bad weather and electrical
equipment like motors can
disrupt the signal and make the
programme sound crackly.

▼ On the outside, digital radios look
similar to other radios. But they are
less prone to crackles and fade-out.

DAB

Digital radio (DAB, digital audio broadcasting)
uses radio waves in a different way. The
signals coming from the transmitter carry
many different programmes all at once, broken
into tiny digital fragments and mixed together
in a coded form, called multiplexing. The
transmitter sends each programme fragment
more than once, so the radio set has more than
one chance to find the pieces it needs. If you
are in a car, signals can reach your digital
radio from different transmitters in different
directions. The radio constantly sorts through
all these incoming digital fragments, thousands
of times each second. It then selects and pieces
together only the programme you want.

DIGITAL TELEVISION

Television uses radio waves
to carry both pictures and
sounds through the air.
Digital television is broadcast
in a similar way to digital
radio, and promises better
picture and sound quality as
well as far more channels.
Some digital TV sets can
'make time stand still'. If you
press the pause button, the set
starts recording the incoming
digital signals automatically
on a hard drive memory
inside. When you press pause
again, the TV plays back the
signals it recorded.

▲ Watching digital TV can be an exciting interactive experience. Using the remote control, viewers can access all kinds of extra information, select and watch different views in small panels on the screen, and listen to the words spoken in various languages.

Digital television broadcasts do not just carry pictures and sounds. They can also transmit background information, such as details about the programme you are watching, and programmes on other channels. You can usually see this by pressing a special button on your digital TV set or remote control.

DIGITAL NETWORKS

With so much digital information bouncing around the world, we need new ways to carry it swiftly and efficiently. Wire cables are still very common. But fibre-optic cables and wireless connections play an increasing role in digital networks.

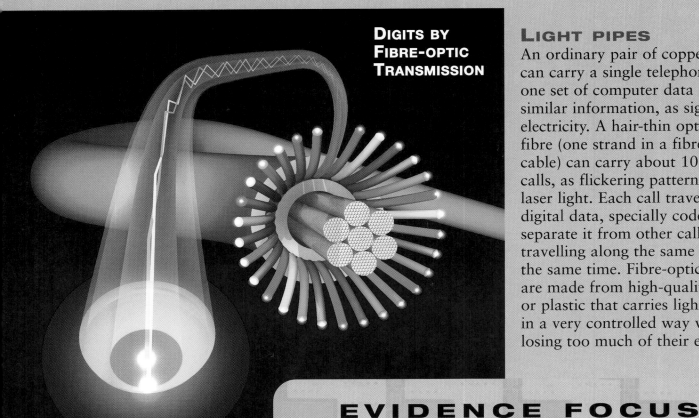

DIGITS BY FIBRE-OPTIC TRANSMISSION

LIGHT PIPES

An ordinary pair of copper wires can carry a single telephone call, one set of computer data or similar information, as signals of electricity. A hair-thin optical fibre (one strand in a fibre-optic cable) can carry about 10 million calls, as flickering patterns of laser light. Each call travels as digital data, specially coded to separate it from other calls travelling along the same fibre at the same time. Fibre-optic cables are made from high-quality glass or plastic that carries light rays in a very controlled way without losing too much of their energy.

▲ Light travels along a single optical fibre by bouncing in a zig-zag pattern off the inner surface (above left). Many fibres are bundled into one fibre-optic cable with a core of metal wires for strength (above right). The glass or plastic of the fibres is strong yet light, and thin enough to bend around corners.

EVIDENCE FOCUS

FIBRE-OPTIC INFORMATION

You need an old plastic water bottle, a torch and an A4-sized piece of cooking foil or dark paper. Do this experiment in a darkened bathroom or kitchen. First fill the bottle with water. Then wrap the foil or paper tightly around it, leaving the top and bottom uncovered. Switch on the torch. Hold it firmly against the bottom of the bottle so its light shines up into the water. Keeping the torch pressed here, slowly tilt the bottle to pour out the water. Notice how the stream of water glows, carrying light rays just like an optical fibre.

INVISIBLE WIRES

Wires and fibre-optic cables carry huge amounts of data. But they can be awkward to install and difficult to move. A more convenient way of sending digital information from place to place is by 'wireless' – radio waves or similar waves such as microwaves. Wireless technology, as used in mobile phones, can send other kinds of information almost instantly.

SHORT-RANGE CONNECTION

Many people are now using wireless technology to link their own computers and other equipment. The digital technology called Bluetooth lets you connect a computer to nearby printers, scanners, cameras and similar devices. Many people also use Bluetooth to connect their mobile phone to a nearby hands-free, wire-free headset.

HOT SPOTS

Wi-Fi (Wireless Fidelity) is a way of linking up an entire computer network using radio waves instead of wires. A radio transmitter-receiver box, or access point, creates an invisible network area around itself called a hot spot. With the right equipment, other computers can connect into this network by being placed inside the hot spot. Travellers use Wi-Fi hot-spots in cafés, libraries, shopping centres, train stations and airports. Their laptop computers or mobile phones can send emails and surf the Web.

▶ Wireless networks mean people can access the Internet more or less anywhere – even on horseback. A special transmitter-receiver in this laptop allows the computer to send and receive information to a local base station in wireless form, by radio waves instead of cables.

▼ This Bluetooth earpiece contains a tiny radio transmitter and receiver. It sends signals to and from a mobile phone or ordinary fixed phone by radio waves, allowing the person to move around easily.

DIGITAL SOCIETY

One view of digital technology is that it allows us to make amazing technical gadgets like computers and mobile phones, which send and receive and process information. Another view is that digital technology gives people the tools to improve their lives.

▲ The digital bar codes on product labels and bank cards could allow people to scan and pay for their own purchases at a store checkout, as here in Germany. At the same time, digitally based closed-circuit TV cameras monitor attempted fraud or theft.

POWER TO THE PEOPLE

Digital technologies give people much more power over information. They let us do many things that we could not do easily before, like being more creative, and helping us to communicate with others. For example, using a computer, synthesiser and digital camera, you could make your own digital books, songs, photos or videos. You could then share these with millions of other people by putting them on your own website.

HISTORY FOCUS

DIGITAL REVOLUTIONS

People are increasingly using digital technologies to help them change their societies. In 1998, the people of Indonesia used the Internet to organise an uprising against their leader, President Suharto. Eventually he was forced out of power. Four years later, people in the Philippines used mobile phones and text messages in a similar way to organise the overthrow of dictator Joseph Estrada.

BLOGGING

A blog is a kind of diary or journal available online over the Internet. It gives people the power to make comments on their own experiences and events which are shared with other people all over the world.

IN TOUCH WITH THE WORLD

Years ago you could find detailed information about certain subjects only by going to a specialist library in a major city. Now, anyone with a computer and Internet access can tap into a universe of digital information – without leaving home.

We can send digital information around the world so quickly and easily that our society is changing fast. Television, radio and the Internet bring us news of dramatic events anywhere on the planet, often as they happen. Thanks to the World Wide Web, we can read today's newspapers, listen to the radio or view television programmes from almost any nation around the world.

THE GLOBAL VILLAGE

More than any other technology, the Internet bridges the divide between countries. It makes the world seem much smaller and more intimate – a 'global village'. This helps people in different countries to understand one another's traditions and cultures. It also allows people to find friends with shared interests all over the world. Whole new 'online communities' form as people look at websites, send emails and chat over the Net.

▼ Mobile satellite trucks like these can broadcast live TV news pictures from anywhere in the world. Many television stations also send news via the Internet, so people can watch on a desktop or laptop computer whenever and wherever they wish.

DIGITAL RIGHTS AND WRONGS

Digital technologies like the Internet help us to enjoy freedoms such as democracy and free speech. But the same technologies can also help people who want to undermine or take away these freedoms.

DIGITAL RIGHTS

Most people in Western countries live in democratic societies where they can speak fairly freely and vote to choose their leaders. This helps people to discuss their political ideas and to campaign for changes that could improve society. The Internet has the power to make us better informed, more thoughtful and more caring. Indeed some people believe the online world of 'cyberspace' is fairer and more humane than the real world. In cyberspace the quality of your ideas matters more than your sex or race, or how much money you have.

Unlike the real world, the Internet currently has no borders. You can visit any part of 'cyberspace' without a passport, chat online with friends in Mongolia or Timbuktu, and search for information on any subject you wish. And you can do all this privately and anonymously, in your own home.

▼ Airports are now using digital technology to recognise people's faces and fingerprints. Although this greatly increases security, some people fear that it reduces their civil liberty – their personal freedom in society.

DIGITAL WRONGS

In the same way that the Internet gives us freedom, so it can take away freedom. Crimes are frequently committed, for example, in online auction rooms or by altering bank accounts. A number of terrorist groups have set up websites to promote their views and find supporters.

Digital technologies like the Internet and mobile phones bring tremendous interconnection – and possible new dangers. Harmful computer programs called viruses and worms can spread around the world in days or even hours, with damage and disruption to computers and mobile phones. As we surf the Internet, websites can collect a great deal of personal information about us and our habits. This can make it difficult to protect our privacy.

▲ Satellites rely on digital technology to give us better weather forecasts, satellite television and satellite navigation (GPS). But they can also be used to take secret photographs of buildings and track the movements of vehicles and even individual people.

EVIDENCE FOCUS

DIGITAL BALANCE SHEET

Take a large sheet of paper and draw a line down the middle to make two columns. Write a plus sign + at the top of the left column and a minus sign – at the top of the right column. In the left column, list all the good or positive features you can think of about digital technology. In the right column, list the bad or negative points. On balance, do you think digital technology is more good than bad?

THE DIGITAL FUTURE

There is little doubt that digital technology is here to stay. Our hectic modern lives rely on convenient gadgets like mobile phones, laptop computers, digital cameras and portable music players. But there are many challenges ahead.

COMING TOGETHER

When words, pictures and sounds are turned into digital form, they can be stored and processed on many different digital gadgets. Some of these are gradually merging. For example, you can take a digital photo with your mobile phone, store photos on your MP3 music player, compose music with your computer and play games on your digital wristwatch. Will we have separate phones, music players, computers and watches in the future? Or just one digital gadget that does everything?

SMART HOMES

You can already use the Internet to control your DVD recorder or burglar alarm while you are on holiday. The latest fridges can pick up digital signals from tiny radio-transmitter tags called RFIDs embedded in items like milk cartons and cheese wrappers. This alerts you when food or drink is getting old, and can even order new supplies over the Internet. Some washing machines have built-in computer chips that weigh your clothes and work out how to use water, detergent and electricity more efficiently. Future 'smart homes' could have a computer system that controls everything from the lights to the blinds, music, television, heating, cooker and even the cat-flap.

▲ Even sports like soccer, American football, tennis or skiing could be digital. In soccer, microchips might be built into the ball and into every player's shinpad. These send signals to a computer that helps the referee to make more accurate decisions, like whether the ball crossed the goal line.

FACT FOCUS

PROBLEMS IN THE MAKING?

- 'Cyber crime' (involving computers) affects one-half of all businesses.

- Spam (unwanted junk email) increases by up to four-fifths each year.

- Nearly two-thirds of shoppers say the Net has reduced their purchases in real shops, affecting shopping areas and people's jobs.

- The authorities in four-fifths of American cities are concerned about a terrorist attack using the Internet.

- Nearly one-quarter of all 15–17 year-old teenagers have used the Internet to cheat at their school work.

▲ This futuristic robot is a 'guard-dog' when you are not at home. If a burglar enters, its built-in sound sensors and digital camera automatically send pictures to your mobile phone.

THE ROAD AHEAD

People are not computers, and 'living by numbers' does not appeal to everyone. We cannot know how digital technologies like the Internet will change society in the long run. Will we spend too much time staring at our computers and too little time having fun with our friends? Many people enjoy some conveniences of modern technology. But they also like the warmth and humanity of older ways of life, like curling up in bed with a book rather than a laptop.

Digital technology is helping us to create, store, process and send ever more quantities of information. But there is a limit to how much we can read, take in or think about each day. We have to ensure that digital technology truly improves the quality of our lives, not just the quantity of information we have to handle.

▶ Digital technology makes it easier for people to work together when they are far apart. But many people still prefer to use 'timeless technologies' like books and face-to-face conversation, which make the real world interesting.

TIMELINE

Here are some of the main discoveries
and milestones in the history of digital
technology and similar areas of science,
such as computers.

THIRD CENTURY BC In Eastern Asia, the Babylonian people devise a number system including a version of zero.

FOURTH CENTURY AD Central American civilisations use the number zero.

FIFTH CENTURY AD In the Indian region, Hindu people independently invent the number zero, which gradually makes its way to the Arabic regions of the Middle East and North Africa, and then to Europe.

1703 Gottfried Leibniz incorporates zero into a new number system, binary, which will eventually be used in electronic computers.

1812 English mathematician Charles Babbage designs a programmable digital computer but does not manage to complete its construction.

1864 British physicist James Clerk Maxwell predicts the existence of radio waves, encouraging engineers to make equipment that uses them.

1894 English physicist Sir Oliver Lodge sends the first message by radio waves, which become known as Hertzian waves after another pioneer of radio, Heinrich Hertz.

1900 The first radio telephone is demonstrated by American engineer Reginald A. Fessenden.

1901 Guglielmo Marconi, an Italian working in England, sends radio messages across the Atlantic Ocean from England to Newfoundland.

1927 American scientist Vannevar Bush develops a complex analogue computer called the Differential Analyser. It is first used in weapons research to predict the path of bullets and missiles.

1927 American telephone engineer Harry Nyquist works out the mathematical basis of sampling.

1938 Konrad Zuse, a German engineer, builds the first programmable binary computer in his parents' living room.

1944 Harvard University mathematician Howard Aiken builds the world's first large-scale digital computer. It was called the Harvard Mark I or the Automatic Sequence-Controlled Calculator (ASCC).

1946 Two US scientists, John Mauchly and J Presper Eckert, develop the world's first general-purpose electronic computer called ENIAC (Electronic Numerical Integrator and Calculator).

1947 John Bardeen, Walter Brattain and William Shockley of the USA develop a miniature 'switch', the transistor, that revolutionises the design of electronic equipment.

1948 Claude Shannon, a US mathematician, outlines his 'information theory' – how to code and send digital information in the most efficient way.

1951 Scientists at Massachusetts Institute of Technology (MIT) develop Whirlwind, the first computer to make proper use of graphics.

1954 Indian physicist Narinder Kapany develops fibre-optic technology.

1957 Launch of the Soviet satellite Sputnik 1 opens the way for fast, worldwide communications using radio signals.

1958 In the USA Jack Kilby and Robert Noyce develop the integrated circuit – IC or microchip – that puts miniaturised transistors and other components onto tiny wafers of silicon.

1959 The giant computer company IBM, International Business Machines, develops computer-aided design (CAD).

1961 Computer graphics are used in the title sequence of the Alfred Hitchcock movie *Vertigo*.

1962 Ivan Sutherland, an American computer scientist, develops the first practical word processing program.

1964 IBM pioneers electronic business with a system to buy airline tickets called SABRE.

1969 The US government's Department of Defense sets up ARPANET, the forerunner of the Internet.

1971 Intel Electronics engineer Ted Hoff invents the world's first microprocessor.

1971 Project Gutenberg, a library of books in digital form, is launched in the United States.

1972 The Club of Rome, a group of academics, runs the first computer prediction of the future, called The Limits to Growth. It foretells a bleak future for humanity.

1973 Bob Metcalfe, an American computer scientist, designs Ethernet, a way to link computers together into powerful local networks.

1973 American engineer Martin Cooper develops the mobile phone.

1975 French inventor Raymond Moreno patents the smart card for cashless electronic payment.

1976 Steve Jobs and Steve Wozniak produce the first user-friendly home computer, the Apple I.

1978 The world's first mobile phone service, AMPS (Analogue Mobile Phone Service), is launched in Chicago, USA.

1981 IBM launches its landmark personal computer, the IBM PC, which sets the trend for many years. It has software written by Microsoft, which was then a small company.

1982 Digital mobile phones arrive with the launch of a popular European system called GSM (Global System for Mobile telecommunications).

1982 The world's most popular CAD system, AutoCAD, is launched.

1983 The Sony and Philips electronics companies launch music CDs (compact discs).

1984 Science-fiction writer William Gibson coins the term 'cyberspace' in his novel *Neuromancer*.

1984 Apple Computer launches the powerful, easy-to-use Macintosh range of computers.

1989 Tim Berners-Lee, a British computer programmer, designs the World Wide Web (www).

1991 Philips launches CD-ROMs (compact disc read-only memories), compact discs that can store all kinds of information in read-only digital form.

1993 US computer programmer Marc Andreessen writes the first user-friendly Web browsing program, Mosaic.

1995 Pixar studios produces the first completely computer-generated animated movie, *Toy Story*.

1995 Broadcast.com was founded to send a choice of radio station programmes online over the Internet, as well as via radio waves. It soon became a multi-billion-dollar business.

1995 Microsoft releases the first version of its Internet Explorer web browser.

1997 IBM supercomputer Deep Blue beats the Russian chess grandmaster Gary Kasparov – the first time a machine has beaten a person at chess.

1997 The technology for Wi-Fi, a form of wireless, is agreed.

1999 Shawn Fanning launches Napster music-sharing service.

2001 Apple unveils a pocket-sized digital music player, the iPod.

2003 The US government sues 1,000 people for illegally swapping MP3 music files using their computers.

2004 One in five American voters selects the US president with computerised voting systems.

2005 Apple reveals a version of its iPod that can play digital videos as well as show digital photos and play digital music tracks.

GLOSSARY

analogue Information that varies continuously in value, rather than in separate steps or stages like digital information.

binary A number system and type of arithmetic that uses only the numbers zero and one, 0 and 1, to represent information. Binary is used by virtually all computers.

bit A binary digit, that is, 0 or 1.

byte A group of bits (binary digits), usually 8 or 16 or 32.

CAD (computer-aided design) A way of designing on a computer screen instead of using pen and paper.

CAM (computer-aided manufacture) Making products using digital technology, like computer-controlled welding robots.

CCD (charge-coupled device) The sensitive 'electronic eye' microchip device inside a digital camera, which converts the incoming light rays into a grid-pattern of tiny dots or pixels.

CD (compact disc) A circular sandwich of metal and plastic that can be used to store music, computer data or other information.

CGI (computer-generated imagery) A way of using computers to draw the separate frames that make up animated movies, videos and television programmes.

cyberspace A way of describing the part-real, part-imaginary world where people meet and exchange information using computers and computer-based communications like the Net.

data The digital information stored, processed, and transmitted by computers and similar equipment.

digital Information that varies in separate steps or stages rather than continuously, usually represented with numbers.

download Copying information (such as movies or music) from another computer or network to your own computer.

DVD (digital versatile/video disc) A circular disc, similar to a CD, used to store movies, sounds, photographs, computer data and almost any other kind of information.

email (electronic mail) A way of sending information from one computer to another.

fibre-optic cable Bundle of hair-thin strands of glass or plastic that carry information in the form of laser light waves. Telephone networks and the Internet use fibre-optic cables.

frame One of the still photographs or images that make up a movie or animation.

frequency The rate at which something changes, like sound waves or electric signals, measured in hertz (Hz). A frequency of 100 Hz means 100 changes each second.

gigabyte An amount of computer memory equal to 1,000 million bytes.

hard drive The main storage device or memory inside a computer.

Internet (Net) The worldwide network of computer systems that people use to send emails, swap computer files such as words and pictures, and browse the World Wide Web.

laser A powerful, precise light source that is used to send digital information along fibre-optic cables or scan (read) CDs and DVDs.

microchip A miniaturised computer or memory store on a tiny wafer or chip of silicon, often no bigger than a fingernail.

microprocessor A type of microchip that contains all the main components of a computer – like a computer on a single chip.

MP3 A way of storing sounds and music in digital format as compressed computer files which take up little room and are quick to send over the Internet. MP3 stands for Motion Picture Experts Group 1 Audio Layer 3, which refers to the scientific group that first devised the technology.

online An activity that involves using the Net. For example, an online auction involves bidding for goods through a website.

packet switching The process of breaking apart emails and other information into tiny packets or parcels, to be sent by different routes over the Internet.

PIN (personal identification number) A security number that a person uses for personal and private information.

pixel (picture element) One of the many tiny units that make up a digital picture.

radio wave A type of electromagnetic energy that can carry information silently and invisibly through space at the speed of light.

RFID (radio frequency identification device) A tiny computer chip that sends out information when asked or 'interrogated' by a reader device nearby.

sampling A way of turning analogue information (such as sound) into digital information (such as an MP3 file) by measuring it at certain time intervals and giving the measurements numbers.

SIM (subscriber identification module) The smart card inside a mobile phone that stores account details, phone numbers and other personal information.

smart card A plastic card with a small built-in computer chip that can be used to store money or personal information. Most credit cards are now smart cards.

upload Copying information (such as a Web page) from your computer to another one or to a network.

Wi-Fi (Wireless Fidelity) A wire-free way of connecting computer equipment to a network or to the Internet using radio waves.

www (World Wide Web) Part of the Net that allows people to share information in the form of easy-to-use Web pages.

FURTHER INFORMATION

Books to read

The Chip: How Two Americans Invented the Microchip and Launched a Revolution by Tom Reid (Random House, 2001)

Communications in Close-up: Global Networks by Ian Graham (Evans, 2003)

Cool Stuff and How it Works by Chris Woodford and others (Dorling Kindersley, 2005)

Fantastic Future by Mike Goldsmith (Scholastic, 2004)

How Stuff Works by Marshall Brain (Hungry Minds, 2002)

Internet and Computer Ethics for Kids by Winn Schartau (Interpact, 2001)

The Internet for Dummies by John R Levine (For Dummies Books, 2003)

Milestones in Modern Science: The First Computers by Guy de la Bédoyère (Evans, 2005)

The Road Ahead by Bill Gates (Penguin, 1999)

TechTV's Catalog of Tomorrow by Andrew Zolli (TechTV, 2002)

Usborne Guide to the Internet by Mairi Mackinnon (Usborne, 2002)

Websites

Kids Domain Computer Connections
www.kidsdomain.com/brain/computer/
lesson.html
Learn about computers and programming.

IEEE Virtual Museum
www.ieee-virtual-museum.org/
Explore the digital revolution online.

How Stuff Works: Electronics
http://electronics.howstuffworks.com/
A behind-the-covers look at many everyday digital technologies.

INDEX